BLUE BROCCOLI AND NANOBOTS

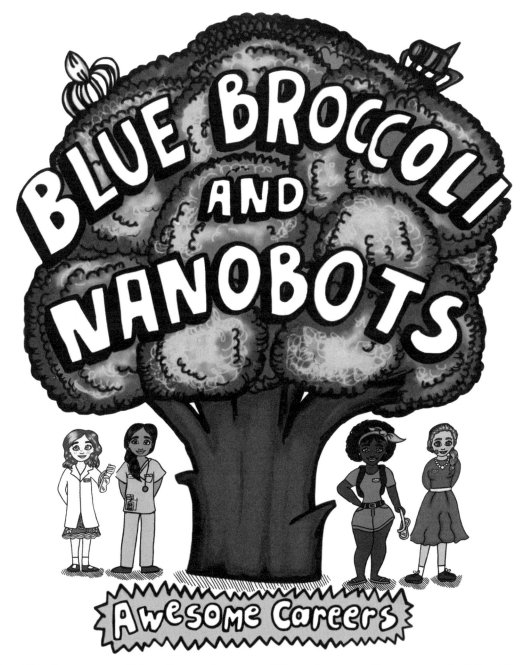

BLUE BROCCOLI AND NANOBOTS

Awesome Careers

in Science, Technology, Engineering and Maths

WRITTEN BY
Bryony Mathew

ILLUSTRATED BY
Millie Bicknelle

CONTENTS

Introduction

By the age of six, many children already believe that girls aren't as clever as boys. They think they're not as good at maths or science. This is just wrong. Early misperceptions about their abilities can have profound effects on girls' self-confidence and discourage them from choosing to study STEM (science, technology, engineering, and maths) subjects in the future.

But the world needs more women in STEM. In the UK alone, only 23 percent of the STEM workforce, and only 14 percent of engineers, are female.

This book is designed as a way for children as young as five to explore future careers in STEM. The aim is not only to challenge the belief that girls aren't as good at science or maths, but to do so at the earliest possible age. I want to get young girls to believe that anything is possible. I want to plant ideas in their minds of jobs they have never even heard of and possibly can't even pronounce on first reading. I want boys to look at this book and see girls being nanotechnologists, aerospace engineers, or theoretical physicists and just think that it's normal. I want both girls and boys to grow up thinking that STEM is for everyone.

This book will open their eyes to a whole new world of opportunities.

Bryony Mathew

SUPER SCIENTISTS

NISHA the NEUROSURGEON

Nisha is a brain doctor. She knows all there is to know about brains. She knows how your brain lets you speak, think, and move, but most importantly, she knows how to fix your brain if something goes wrong.

Brains are made up of tiny little cells called neurons. Neurons in the brain are connected to other nerve cells all through the body. The network of cells is called the nervous system.

Nisha can also fix other parts of the body which connect to the brain, like nerves in the spinal cord, which run right up your back.

Do you like...

☐ Closing your eyes really tight and trying to see inside your head?

☐ Pretending to be a doctor and carefully putting bandages on?

☐ Making brain-shaped jellies?

then you might like to be a neurosurgeon!

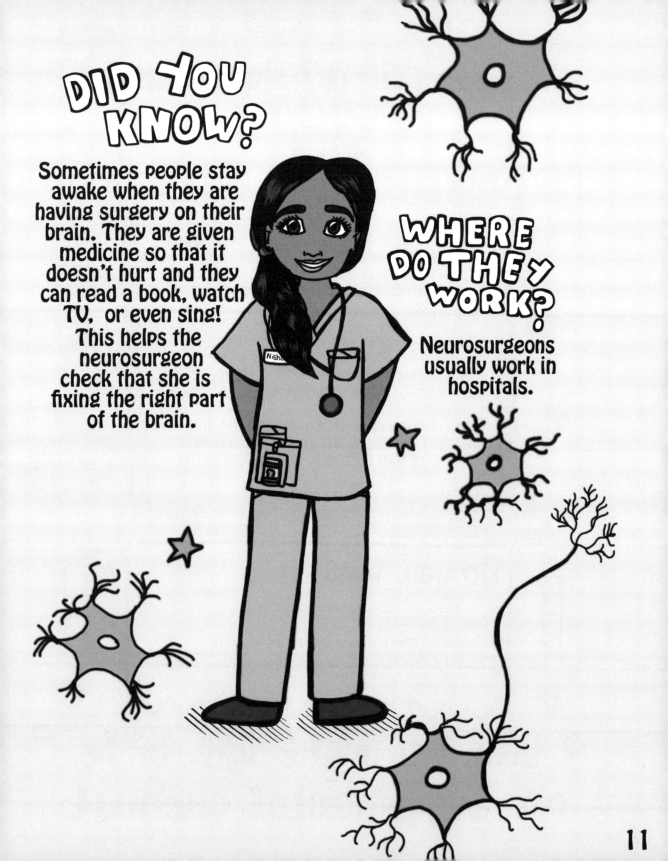

DID YOU KNOW?

Sometimes people stay awake when they are having surgery on their brain. They are given medicine so that it doesn't hurt and they can read a book, watch TV, or even sing! This helps the neurosurgeon check that she is fixing the right part of the brain.

WHERE DO THEY WORK?

Neurosurgeons usually work in hospitals.

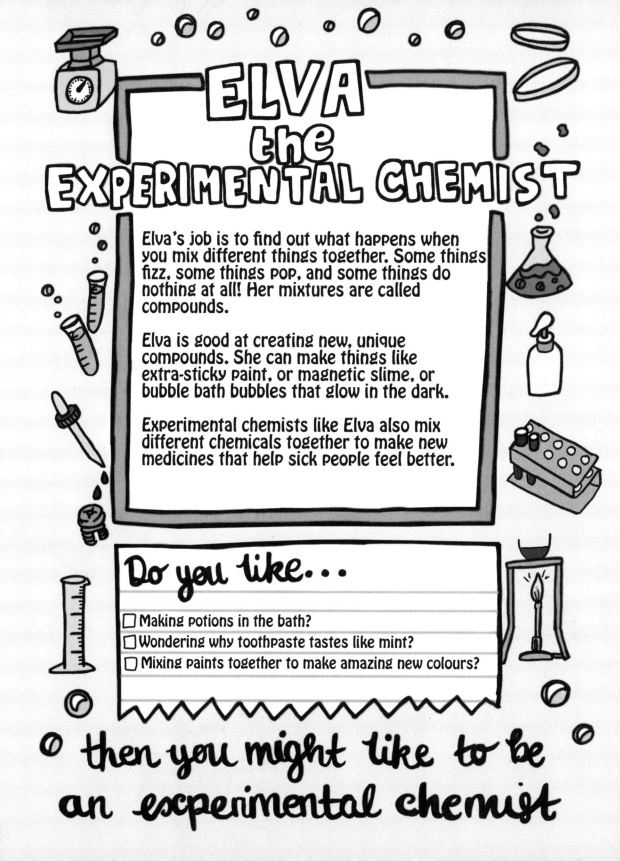

ELVA the EXPERIMENTAL CHEMIST

Elva's job is to find out what happens when you mix different things together. Some things fizz, some things pop, and some things do nothing at all! Her mixtures are called compounds.

Elva is good at creating new, unique compounds. She can make things like extra-sticky paint, or magnetic slime, or bubble bath bubbles that glow in the dark.

Experimental chemists like Elva also mix different chemicals together to make new medicines that help sick people feel better.

Do you like...

☐ Making potions in the bath?
☐ Wondering why toothpaste tastes like mint?
☐ Mixing paints together to make amazing new colours?

then you might like to be an ~~escperimental~~ chemist

DID YOU KNOW?

Experimental chemists can even design medicine for one specific person. It's a bit like measuring someone's feet so that you can make them shoes that fit perfectly.

WHERE DO THEY WORK?

Experimental chemists normally work in laboratories.

FREYA the FORENSIC SCIENTIST

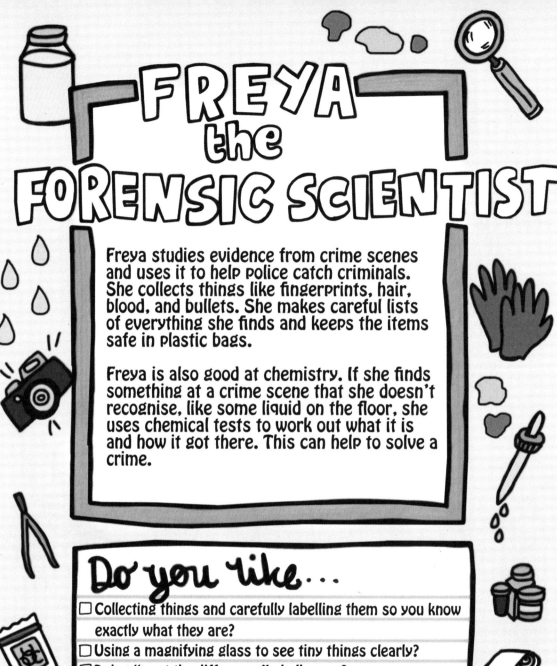

Freya studies evidence from crime scenes and uses it to help police catch criminals. She collects things like fingerprints, hair, blood, and bullets. She makes careful lists of everything she finds and keeps the items safe in plastic bags.

Freya is also good at chemistry. If she finds something at a crime scene that she doesn't recognise, like some liquid on the floor, she uses chemical tests to work out what it is and how it got there. This can help to solve a crime.

Do you like....

☐ Collecting things and carefully labelling them so you know exactly what they are?

☐ Using a magnifying glass to see tiny things clearly?

☐ Doing "spot the difference" challenges?

then you might like to be a forensic scientist

DID YOU KNOW?

Forensic scientists sometimes go to court and tell a judge all about what they found at a crime scene.

This is called being an "expert witness" and it helps the judge decide who is guilty of a crime.

WHERE DO THEY WORK?

Forensic scientists go to wherever a crime has taken place. They might go into a shop, out to a park, or into someone's house.

Freya

JOSIE the OCEANOGRAPHER

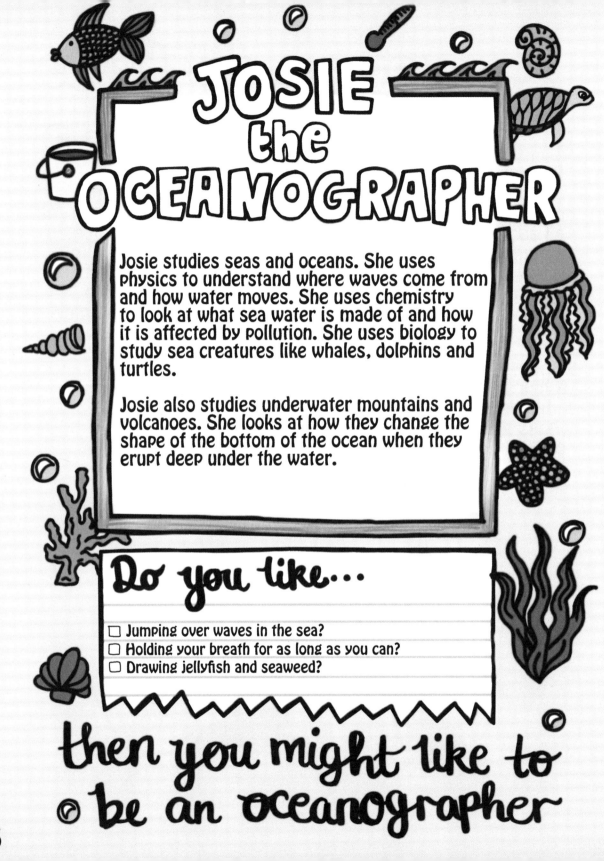

Josie studies seas and oceans. She uses physics to understand where waves come from and how water moves. She uses chemistry to look at what sea water is made of and how it is affected by pollution. She uses biology to study sea creatures like whales, dolphins and turtles.

Josie also studies underwater mountains and volcanoes. She looks at how they change the shape of the bottom of the ocean when they erupt deep under the water.

Do you like...

☐ Jumping over waves in the sea?
☐ Holding your breath for as long as you can?
☐ Drawing jellyfish and seaweed?

then you might like to be an oceanographer

DID YOU KNOW?

Oceanographers go on exciting expeditions to seas and oceans all over the world.

They collect samples and bring them back home to study.

WHERE DO THEY WORK?

Oceanographers work in laboratories, at sea on offshore platforms, or on research ships out on the ocean.

THEA
the
THEORETICAL PHYSICIST

Thea's job is to try to understand how nature works. She uses maths to answer questions like, "Why is the sky blue?" and "Why do stars shine?"

Thea can tell us how volcanoes explode, why earthquakes make the ground shake, and how hurricanes happen.

To answer these questions, Thea studies elementary particles. These are the most basic parts of natural forces like gravity.

By understanding these tiny particles, theoretical physicists like Thea are helping us to understand the world we live in.

$$\nabla \times E = \frac{\partial B}{\partial t}$$

$$\nabla \cdot B = 0$$

$$\nabla \cdot D = \rho_f$$

$$\nabla \times H = J + \frac{\partial D}{\partial t}$$

Do you like...

☐ Lying on the grass in the summer and wondering why the sky above you is blue?

☐ Trying to count the stars in the sky at night and wondering why some are brighter than others?

then you might like to be a theoretical physicist

DID YOU KNOW?

The first theoretical physicist was a man named Isaac Newton. He invented whole new ways of doing maths, like calculus, which helped him understand how gravity works.

$$\nabla \times E = \frac{\partial B}{\partial t}$$

$$\nabla \cdot B = 0$$

$$\nabla \cdot D = \rho_f$$

$$\nabla \times H = J_f + \frac{\partial D}{\partial t}$$

WHERE DO THEY WORK?

One of the most famous places where physicists work is called CERN, the European Organisation for Nuclear Research. CERN has special machines that physicists can use to make tiny particles collide with eachother at the speed of light.

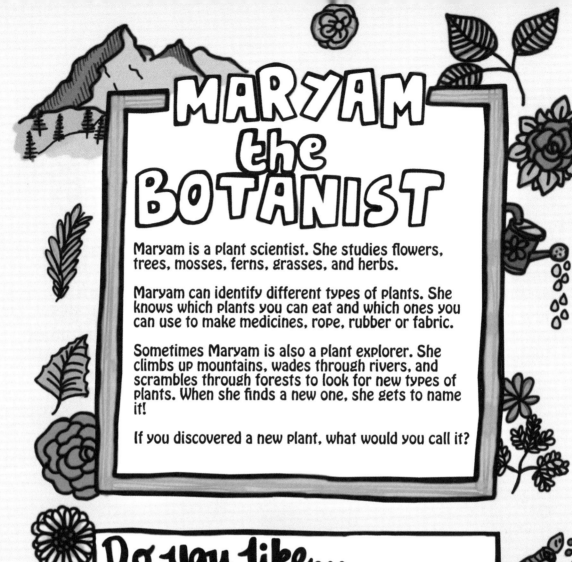

MARYAM the BOTANIST

Maryam is a plant scientist. She studies flowers, trees, mosses, ferns, grasses, and herbs.

Maryam can identify different types of plants. She knows which plants you can eat and which ones you can use to make medicines, rope, rubber or fabric.

Sometimes Maryam is also a plant explorer. She climbs up mountains, wades through rivers, and scrambles through forests to look for new types of plants. When she finds a new one, she gets to name it!

If you discovered a new plant, what would you call it?

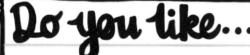

Do you like...

☐ Smelling flowers and climbing trees?
☐ Planting seeds and watching them grow?
☐ Watering the garden?

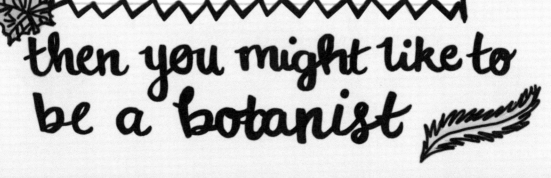

then you might like to be a botanist

DID YOU KNOW?

The biggest flower in the world is called the titan arum. It can grow even taller than an elephant!

WHERE DO THEY WORK?

Botanists work in botanic gardens, universities, and research institutes.

Some spend most of their time outside searching for new plants. Others spend most of their time inside looking at plants under microscopes.

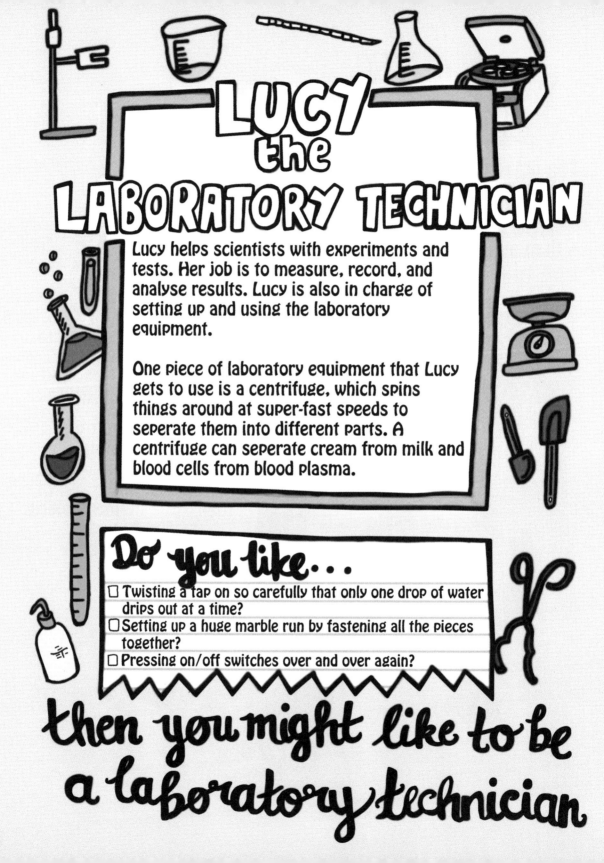

LUCY the LABORATORY TECHNICIAN

Lucy helps scientists with experiments and tests. Her job is to measure, record, and analyse results. Lucy is also in charge of setting up and using the laboratory equipment.

One piece of laboratory equipment that Lucy gets to use is a centrifuge, which spins things around at super-fast speeds to seperate them into different parts. A centrifuge can seperate cream from milk and blood cells from blood plasma.

Do you like...

☐ Twisting a tap on so carefully that only one drop of water drips out at a time?
☐ Setting up a huge marble run by fastening all the pieces together?
☐ Pressing on/off switches over and over again?

then you might like to be a laboratory technician

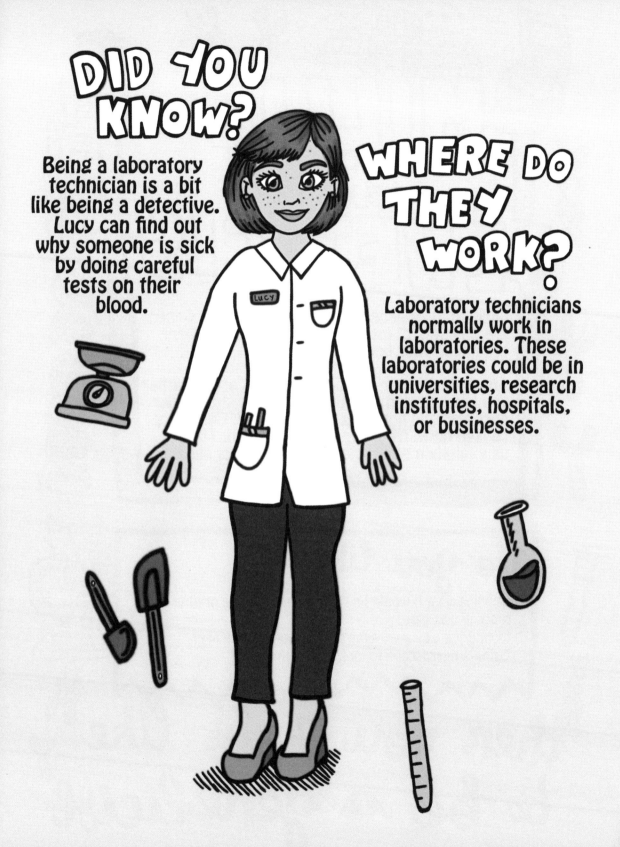

DID YOU KNOW?

Being a laboratory technician is a bit like being a detective. Lucy can find out why someone is sick by doing careful tests on their blood.

WHERE DO THEY WORK?

Laboratory technicians normally work in laboratories. These laboratories could be in universities, research institutes, hospitals, or businesses.

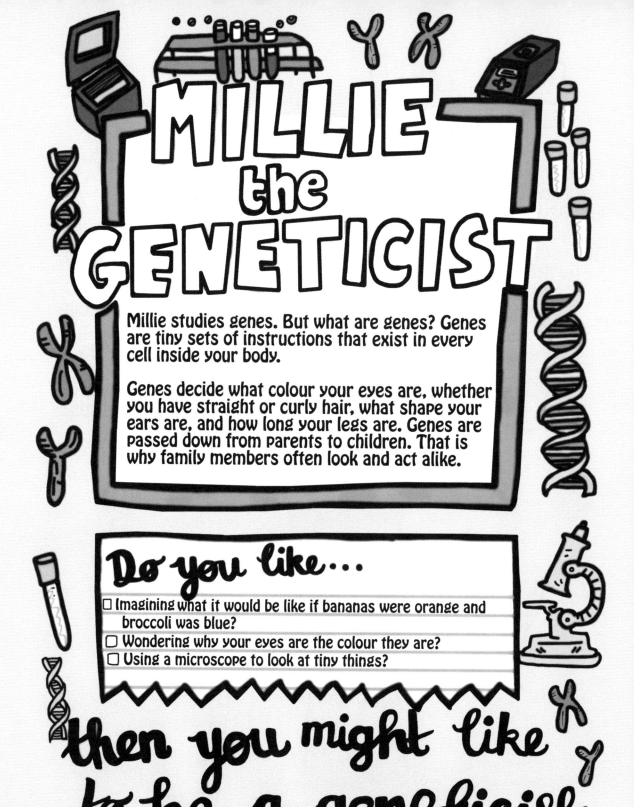

MILLIE the GENETICIST

Millie studies genes. But what are genes? Genes are tiny sets of instructions that exist in every cell inside your body.

Genes decide what colour your eyes are, whether you have straight or curly hair, what shape your ears are, and how long your legs are. Genes are passed down from parents to children. That is why family members often look and act alike.

Do you like...

☐ Imagining what it would be like if bananas were orange and broccoli was blue?
☐ Wondering why your eyes are the colour they are?
☐ Using a microscope to look at tiny things?

then you might like to be a geneticist

DID YOU KNOW?

Geneticists can make plants grow bigger or change colour by changing their genes.

WHERE DO THEY WORK?

Geneticists usually work in laboratories.

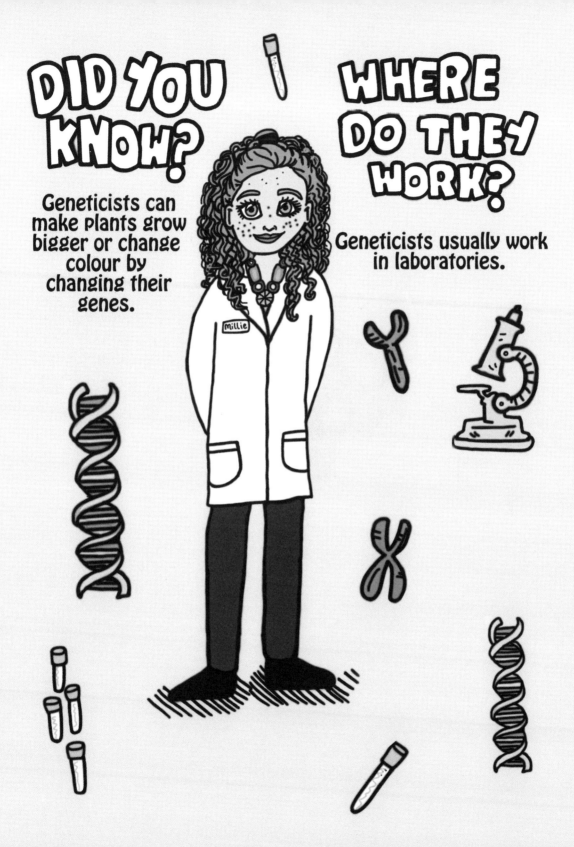

TERRIFIC TECHNOLOGISTS

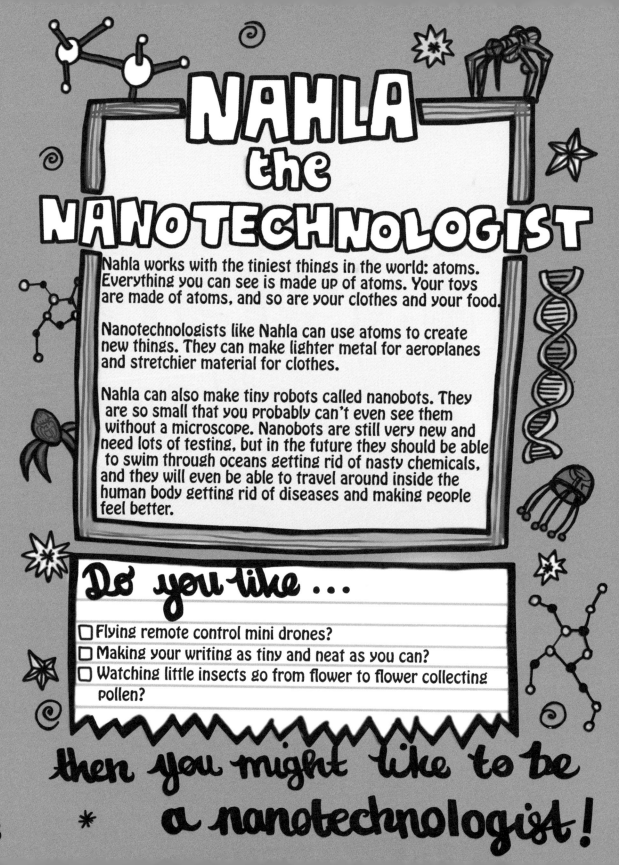

NAHLA the NANOTECHNOLOGIST

Nahla works with the tiniest things in the world: atoms. Everything you can see is made up of atoms. Your toys are made of atoms, and so are your clothes and your food.

Nanotechnologists like Nahla can use atoms to create new things. They can make lighter metal for aeroplanes and stretchier material for clothes.

Nahla can also make tiny robots called nanobots. They are so small that you probably can't even see them without a microscope. Nanobots are still very new and need lots of testing, but in the future they should be able to swim through oceans getting rid of nasty chemicals, and they will even be able to travel around inside the human body getting rid of diseases and making people feel better.

Do you like ...

- ☐ Flying remote control mini drones?
- ☐ Making your writing as tiny and neat as you can?
- ☐ Watching little insects go from flower to flower collecting pollen?

then you might like to be a nanotechnologist!

Nanotechnologists are new! We didn't have miscroscopes strong enough to see atoms until 1981. These are called Scanning Tunneling Microscopes (STM).

WHERE DO THEY WORK?

Nanotechologists work in laboratories. They spend a lot of time working with microscopes and computers.

29

MOLLY the METROLOGIST

Molly's job is to make sure things are measured properly. She can measure all sorts of different things like length, weight, electric currents, temperatures and time. Sometimes Molly will work on developing a new clock. Other times she might check that petrol pumps are pumping out the right amount of petrol, or make sure the lines on measuring jugs are in just the right place.

Molly works together with other metrologists around the world to come up with new ways of making measurements. She also checks that different measurement units (like metres and kilograms) are the same size in every country. This way, people living in different countries can work together well because their technologies fit together.

Do you like...

☐ Making sure that all the clocks in your house tell the right time?
☐ Trying to make a see-saw balance by carefully arranging which friends should sit on which end?
☐ Using a thermometer to measure your temperature?

then you might like to be a metrologist

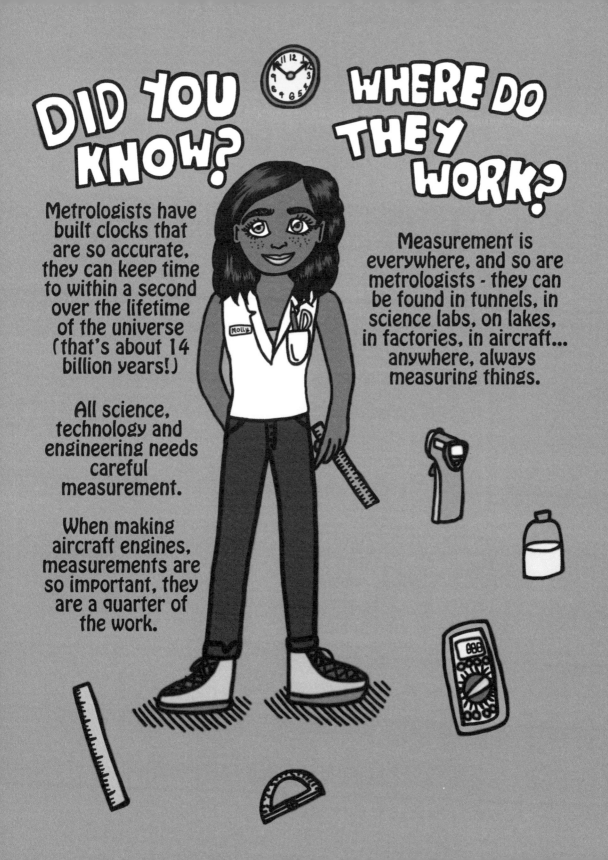

DID YOU KNOW?

WHERE DO THEY WORK?

Metrologists have built clocks that are so accurate, they can keep time to within a second over the lifetime of the universe (that's about 14 billion years!)

All science, technology and engineering needs careful measurement.

When making aircraft engines, measurements are so important, they are a quarter of the work.

Measurement is everywhere, and so are metrologists - they can be found in tunnels, in science labs, on lakes, in factories, in aircraft... anywhere, always measuring things.

DALIA
the
COMPUTER-AIDED DESIGN TECHNICIAN

Dalia uses special computer programmes to make careful digital drawings that show exactly how a machine or building should be put together. Sometimes Dalia will even make models to show what a machine or building would look like in real life.

When she has finished designing, Dalia gives her drawings and models to engineers who build what she has designed!

Do you like...

☐ Using a ruler to draw pictures?
☐ Imagining building a house on the moon?
☐ Measuring how big things are?

then you might like to be a computer-aided design technician

DID YOU KNOW?

Computer Aided Design technicians use the computer mouse and keyboard to draw lines and shapes on the computer.

This makes it easy for them to make changes as they draw.

WHERE DO THEY WORK?

Computer Aided Design technicians can work in different places like factories, offices, and construction sites. They usually work as part of a team together with other technicians and engineers.

33

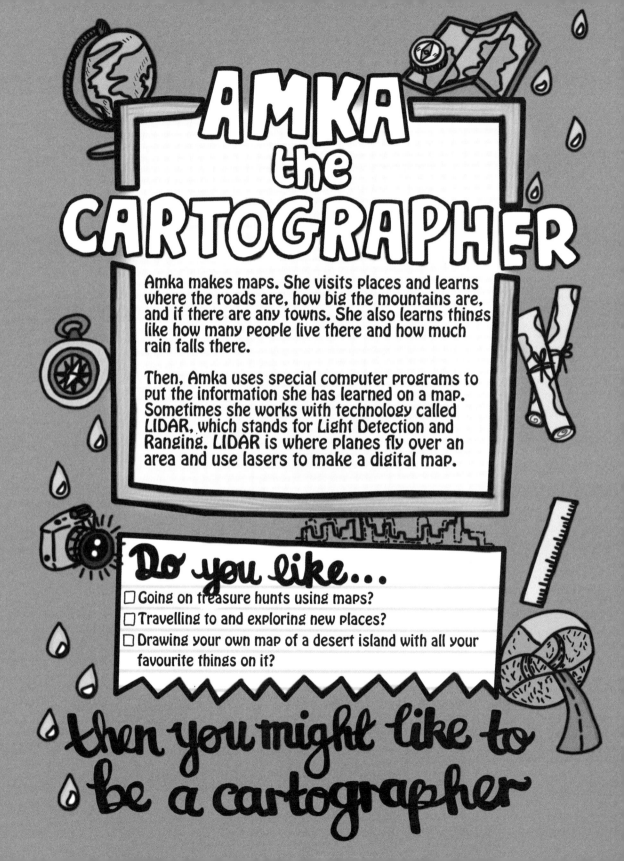

AMKA the CARTOGRAPHER

Amka makes maps. She visits places and learns where the roads are, how big the mountains are, and if there are any towns. She also learns things like how many people live there and how much rain falls there.

Then, Amka uses special computer programs to put the information she has learned on a map. Sometimes she works with technology called LIDAR, which stands for Light Detection and Ranging. LIDAR is where planes fly over an area and use lasers to make a digital map.

Do you like...

☐ Going on treasure hunts using maps?

☐ Travelling to and exploring new places?

☐ Drawing your own map of a desert island with all your favourite things on it?

then you might like to be a cartographer

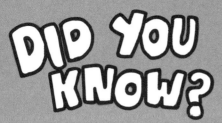

DID YOU KNOW?

WHERE DO THEY WORK?

The first maps were made hundreds of years ago using brushes on an old type of paper called parchment.

Cartographers spend a lot of time in offices working on computers. They also go out in the field to collect new information.

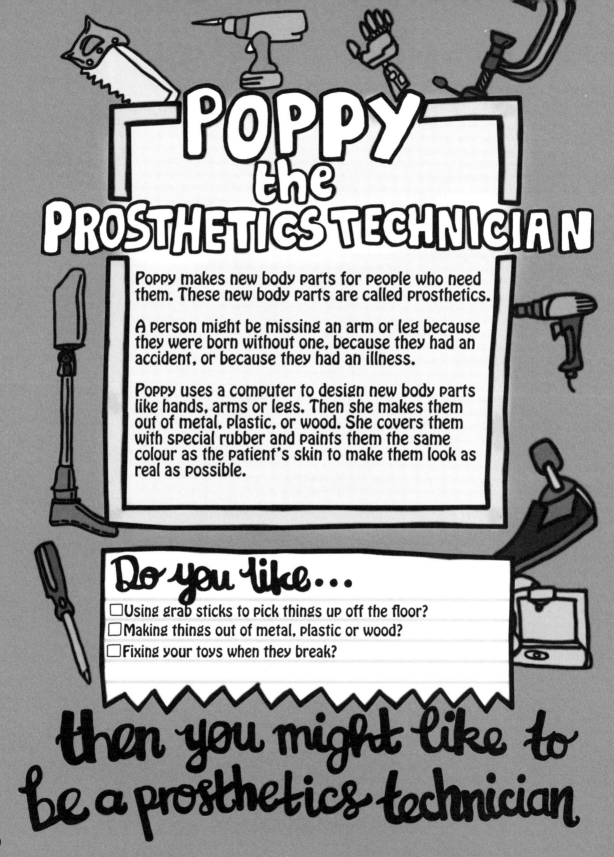

POPPY the PROSTHETICS TECHNICIAN

Poppy makes new body parts for people who need them. These new body parts are called prosthetics.

A person might be missing an arm or leg because they were born without one, because they had an accident, or because they had an illness.

Poppy uses a computer to design new body parts like hands, arms or legs. Then she makes them out of metal, plastic, or wood. She covers them with special rubber and paints them the same colour as the patient's skin to make them look as real as possible.

Do you like...

☐ Using grab sticks to pick things up off the floor?
☐ Making things out of metal, plastic or wood?
☐ Fixing your toys when they break?

then you might like to be a prosthetics technician

DID YOU KNOW?

There are also some special sports prosthetics which are designed to help people run as fast as possible.

These ones don't look anything like real legs, they are amazing flexible blades!

WHERE DO THEY WORK?

Prosthetics technicians usually work in hospitals or health clinics. They work with doctors and nurses.

SUKI the CYBER SECURITY ANALYST

Cyber is another word for computer network. Suki's job is to keep computer networks safe. Imagine that computer networks are like castles. Suki is like a knight who protects the castle from people who want to get in.

If a company is designing an amazing new car and they don't want anyone to steal their design, they need a cyber security analyst like Suki. She makes sure that a company's systems and information are secure and that no-one can find out their secret plans.

Do you like...

☐ Typing passwords into a computer?
☐ Making up code words to share with your friends?
☐ Using padlocks to keep your things safe?

then you might like to be a cyber security analyst

38

DID YOU KNOW?

The world needs more cyber security analysts! Right now, there aren't enough to go around.

WHERE DO THEY WORK?

Cyber security analysts work in businesses, universities, governments, schools, libraries, and other places with computer systems.

PHOEBE the PACKAGING TECHNOLOGIST

Phoebe makes packaging like milk cartons, cereal boxes, and shampoo bottles. She uses computers to draw her designs and then makes real-life versions to test them.

Sometimes, the packages leak, or get squashed too easily, or are hard to open. Then Phoebe goes back to the computer and changes the design.

When she's got it just right, Phoebe works with artists to decide what pictures to put on the packaging. She wants to make it look as good as possible so that people will want to buy the product.

Do you like...

- ☐ Trying to fit as many marshmallows as you can in your mouth at once?
- ☐ Wrapping up presents?
- ☐ Carefully pouring water out of one bottle and into another?

then you might like to be a packaging technologist

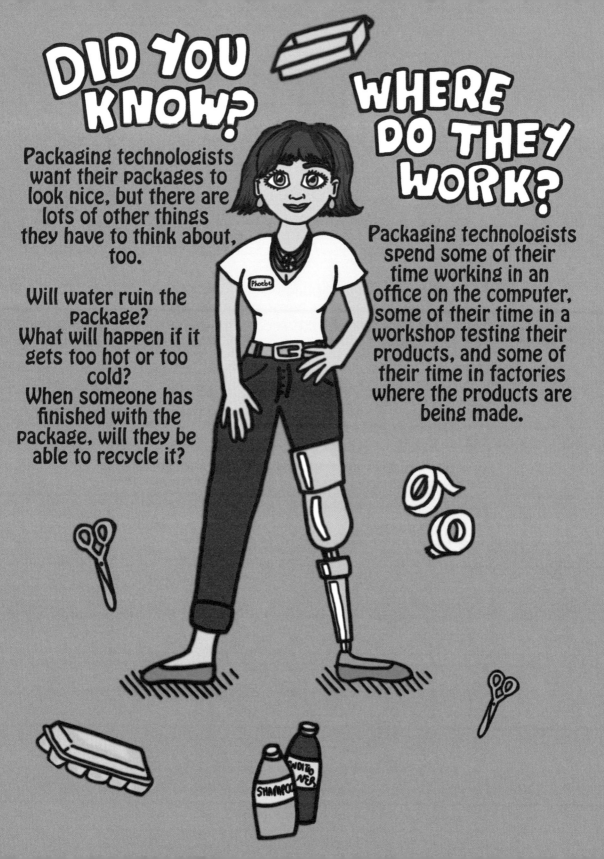

DID YOU KNOW?

Packaging technologists want their packages to look nice, but there are lots of other things they have to think about, too.

Will water ruin the package?
What will happen if it gets too hot or too cold?
When someone has finished with the package, will they be able to recycle it?

WHERE DO THEY WORK?

Packaging technologists spend some of their time working in an office on the computer, some of their time in a workshop testing their products, and some of their time in factories where the products are being made.

41

LI-NA the WEB DEVELOPER

Li Na designs and builds websites. She is good at computer programming and can write code in different programming languages like Java and BASIC.

Li Na also has an artistic mind. She knows what makes a website look exciting. She also thinks carefully about how to make her websites easy for people to use.

Do you like...

- ☐ Searching for new information on the internet?
- ☐ Designing your own mazes and getting your friends to try to find the best way out?
- ☐ Drawing pictures on a computer?

then you might like to be a web developer?

DID YOU KNOW?

There are lots of websites, but not enough web developers. That means there are lots of job opportunities for people who want to make websites.

WHERE DO THEY WORK?

Web developers normally work in offices. But they can also work from their homes as long as they have a computer and internet access.

WWW.

WWW

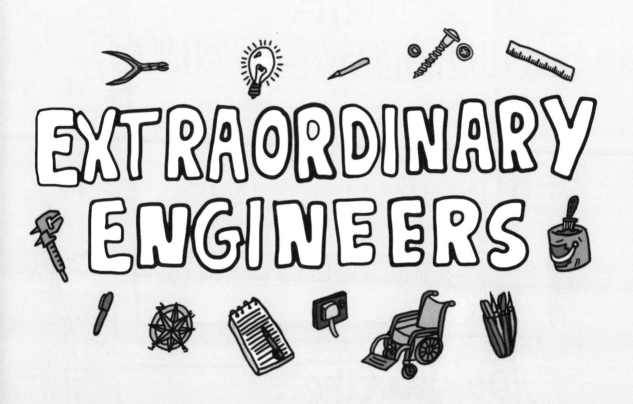

EXTRAORDINARY ENGINEERS

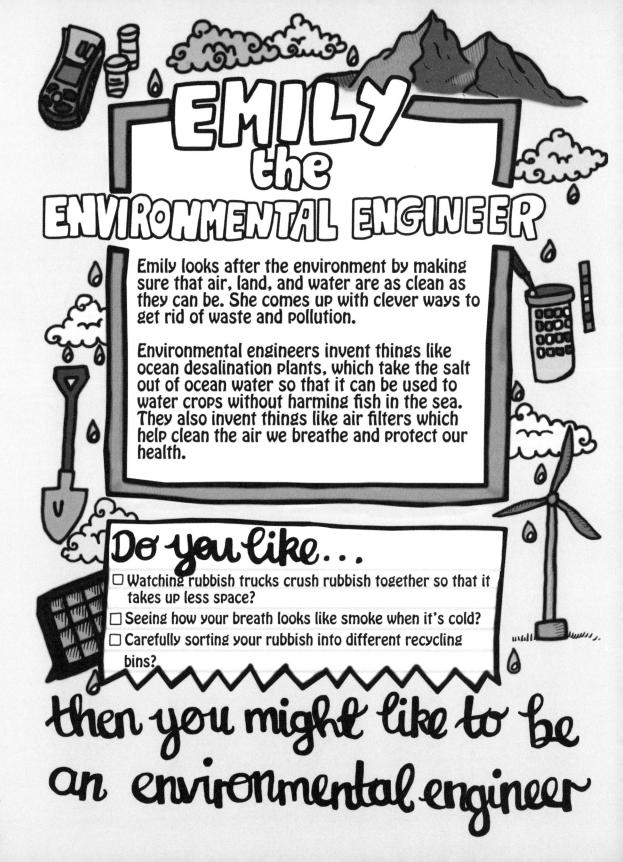

EMILY the ENVIRONMENTAL ENGINEER

Emily looks after the environment by making sure that air, land, and water are as clean as they can be. She comes up with clever ways to get rid of waste and pollution.

Environmental engineers invent things like ocean desalination plants, which take the salt out of ocean water so that it can be used to water crops without harming fish in the sea. They also invent things like air filters which help clean the air we breathe and protect our health.

Do you like...

☐ Watching rubbish trucks crush rubbish together so that it takes up less space?

☐ Seeing how your breath looks like smoke when it's cold?

☐ Carefully sorting your rubbish into different recycling bins?

then you might like to be an environmental engineer

46

DID YOU KNOW?

Environmental engineers help make sure that everyone has access to clean air, water, and food. Now that there are so many people on Earth, the enviromental engineer's job is more important than ever.

WHERE DO THEY WORK?

Environmental engineers usually work in offices, but sometimes they go out in the field.

AALIYAH the AEROSPACE ENGINEER

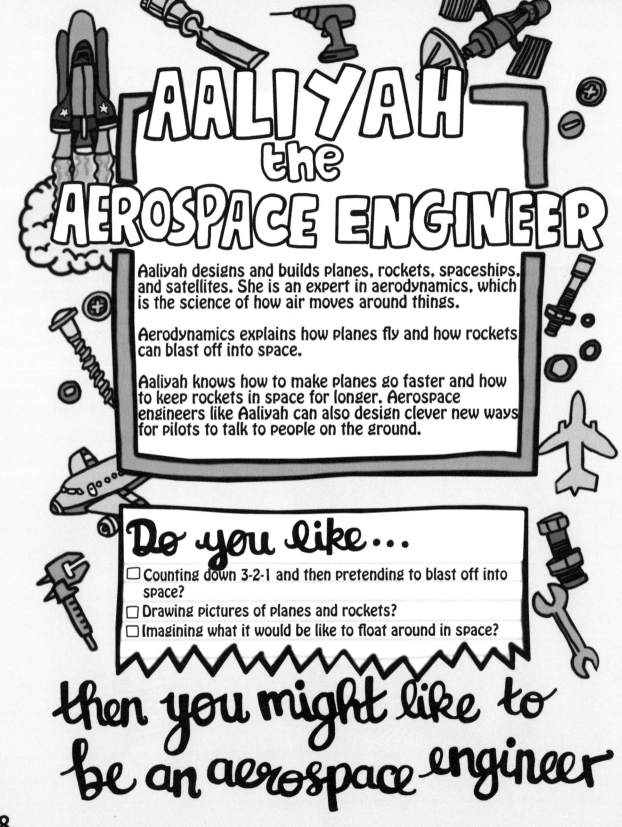

Aaliyah designs and builds planes, rockets, spaceships, and satellites. She is an expert in aerodynamics, which is the science of how air moves around things.

Aerodynamics explains how planes fly and how rockets can blast off into space.

Aaliyah knows how to make planes go faster and how to keep rockets in space for longer. Aerospace engineers like Aaliyah can also design clever new ways for pilots to talk to people on the ground.

Do you like...

☐ Counting down 3-2-1 and then pretending to blast off into space?

☐ Drawing pictures of planes and rockets?

☐ Imagining what it would be like to float around in space?

then you might like to be an aerospace engineer

DID YOU KNOW?

Aerospace engineers are often called rocket scientists.

WHERE DO THEY WORK?

Aerospace engineers work in offices, laboratories, or workshops. Some of them work for companies, some of them for research institutes, and some of them work for the government.

LAYLA
the
BOAT BUILDER

Can you guess what Layla the boat builder does? You've got it: she builds boats! Layla is like a carpenter, electrician, plumber, welder, and painter all in one, and she uses all these skills to build boats. She can work on little sailing boats, big yachts, and huge cruise ships.

Layla starts by deciding what the boat will look like. Then she builds the frame, the hull (the bottom of the boat), the deck, and the cabins. If it's a sailing boat, she fastens on a mast and strong sails. If it has an engine, she carefully fits the engine into the right place. Layla always makes sure she tests the boat on water to check that it works properly.

Do you like...

☐ Carefully placing things on water to see whether they float?

☐ Sailing on the ocean?

☐ Climbing inside boats to see what they have inside?

then you might like to be a boat builder

DID YOU KNOW?

Some boats can cut through ice! These are called icebreakers, and they have sharp edges at the front of the boat that can slide through thick ice.

Sailors use them to travel to very cold places like Greenland and Antarctica.

WHERE DO THEY WORK?

Boat builders work in boatyards, which are like factories just for boats.

Layla

ROSIE the ROBOTICS ENGINEER

Rosie makes robots. First, she thinks of what the robot needs to do. Then, she uses her computer to design what the robot will look like and to program how it will do what she needs it to do.

Robotics engineers like Rosie work with scientists to design robots that can help fix spaceships in outer space and robots that can help doctors perform surgery. They make robot dogs that can walk and bark and robot cameras that can climb walls or fly. Some robotics engineers work for the military making robots that can go into unsafe places so that people don't have to be in danger.

Do you like ...

☐ Playing with robots?

☐ Racing remote control cars?

☐ Imagining what it would be like if your very own robot brought you breakfast in bed each morning?

then you might like to be a robotics engineer!

DID YOU KNOW?

Making a robot is difficult and can take a lot of time. Robotics engineers like Rosie need to be very patient.

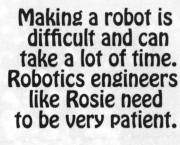

WHERE DO THEY WORK?

Robotics engineers spend some of their time in laboratories and some of their time in offices.

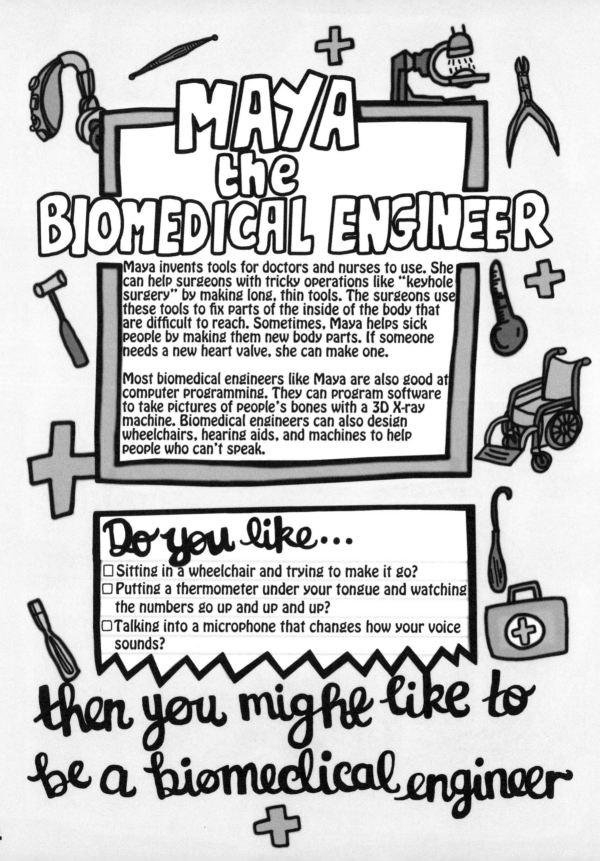

MAYA the BIOMEDICAL ENGINEER

Maya invents tools for doctors and nurses to use. She can help surgeons with tricky operations like "keyhole surgery" by making long, thin tools. The surgeons use these tools to fix parts of the inside of the body that are difficult to reach. Sometimes, Maya helps sick people by making them new body parts. If someone needs a new heart valve, she can make one.

Most biomedical engineers like Maya are also good at computer programming. They can program software to take pictures of people's bones with a 3D X-ray machine. Biomedical engineers can also design wheelchairs, hearing aids, and machines to help people who can't speak.

Do you like...

☐ Sitting in a wheelchair and trying to make it go?
☐ Putting a thermometer under your tongue and watching the numbers go up and up and up?
☐ Talking into a microphone that changes how your voice sounds?

then you might like to be a biomedical engineer

DID YOU KNOW?

Every time you go to the doctor, you see things made by biomedical engineers. They designed the machine that measures your blood pressure, the tool that listens to your heart, and the thermometer that measures your temperature.

WHERE DO THEY WORK?

Biomedical engineers work in hospitals, medical centres, universities, and engineering workshops.

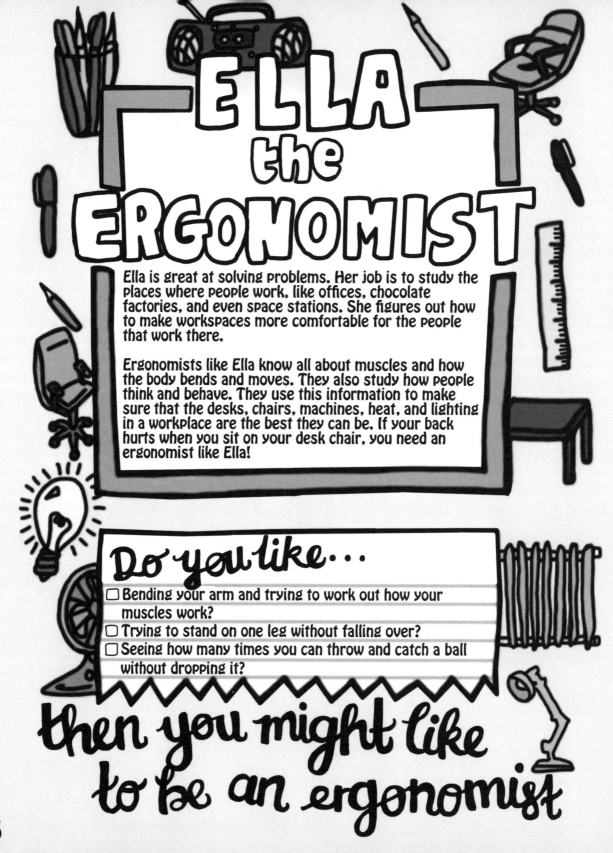

ELLA the ERGONOMIST

Ella is great at solving problems. Her job is to study the places where people work, like offices, chocolate factories, and even space stations. She figures out how to make workspaces more comfortable for the people that work there.

Ergonomists like Ella know all about muscles and how the body bends and moves. They also study how people think and behave. They use this information to make sure that the desks, chairs, machines, heat, and lighting in a workplace are the best they can be. If your back hurts when you sit on your desk chair, you need an ergonomist like Ella!

Do you like...

☐ Bending your arm and trying to work out how your muscles work?
☐ Trying to stand on one leg without falling over?
☐ Seeing how many times you can throw and catch a ball without dropping it?

then you might like to be an ergonomist

Ergonomists like Ella have one big goal: to help hardworking people stay safe and comfortable.

WHERE DO THEY WORK?

Ergonomists can work anywhere! They often work as consultants, which means they have their own offices, but they spend lots of time visiting interesting places like oil rigs, factories, construction sites, hospitals, and train stations.

57

CHLOE the CIVIL ENGINEER

Chloe is in charge of big building projects. She builds things like airports, roads, bridges, tunnels, and skyscrapers. Everyone benefits from the things she makes.

Civil engineers like Chloe have to be very organised and good at working with lots of different people. They need to make sure that all the work is completed in the right order, that it costs the right amount of money, and that there are enough people working so that the project is done on time.

Do you like...

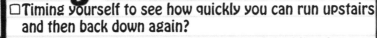

- ☐ Timing yourself to see how quickly you can run upstairs and then back down again?
- ☐ Carefully counting out your money and deciding how much you can spend?
- ☐ Being the leader?

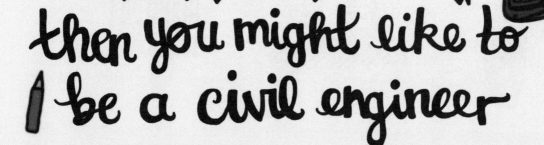

then you might like to be a civil engineer

DID YOU KNOW?

In the 1950s, a civil engineer named Joseph Bazalgette saved the city of London from a dangerous disease called cholera.

Cholera was spreading through dirty water and killing a lot of people. So Joseph Bazalgette designed a new system of sewers that stopped cholera from spreading.

WHERE DO THEY WORK?

Civil engineers spend some of their time in offices and some of their time at building sites. For example, if Chloe is in charge of building an airport, she will spend a lot of time at that airport.

Chloe

CLARA the BROADCAST ENGINEER

Clara helps make TV and radio programmes the best they can be. She is in charge of making sure that TV shows come on at the right time and that the sound on radio programmes is clear and crisp.

Broadcast engineers like Clara set up the electrical equipment that edits and transmits programmes, and they make repairs when things break. They also work on podcasts and on live performances like concerts.

Do you like...

☐ Using walkie-talkies?
☐ Twisting the knob on a really old radio until you can hear what people are saying?
☐ Pretending your hairbrush is a microphone and singing loudly?

then you might like to be a broadcast engineer

DID YOU KNOW?

Have you ever watched a TV programme where they ask you to vote for your favourite person to win a competition? A broadcast engineer like Clara sets up the technology to make that happen.

WHERE DO THEY WORK?

Broadcast engineers usually work in TV and radio studios.

MAGNIFICENT MATHEMATICIANS

AMELIE the ALGORITHM SPECIALIST

Amelie designs new algorithms. But what are algorithms? Algorithms are sets of instructions that tell computers exactly what steps to take in order to solve problems or complete tasks.

You can try making your own algorithm by writing down every step needed to make a jam sandwich. If you can give your instructions to a friend and they can follow them exactly, then you've written a good algorithm! But you need to remember to include every single step. Imagine if you forgot to tell them to take the lid off the jam jar!

Do you like...

Carefully following a recipe to make a delicious chocolate cake?

Playing follow the leader and copying exactly what your friend does?

Writing clues for a treasure hunt?

then you might like to be an algorithm specialist

DID YOU KNOW?

Every time you use Google to search for something on the internet, you are using an algorithm. Google uses an algorithm called PageRank, which decides how important a web page is by looking at the words and links on the page.

WHERE DO THEY WORK?

An algorithm specialist spends most of her time working on a computer. That computer can be anywhere: in an office, at a university, or even at home.

GABRIELLA
the
GEOPHYSICAL MATHEMATICIAN

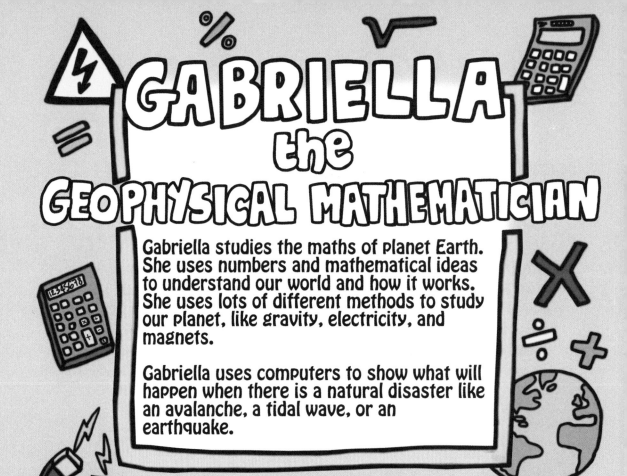

Gabriella studies the maths of planet Earth. She uses numbers and mathematical ideas to understand our world and how it works. She uses lots of different methods to study our planet, like gravity, electricity, and magnets.

Gabriella uses computers to show what will happen when there is a natural disaster like an avalanche, a tidal wave, or an earthquake.

Do you like...

- ☐ Trying to make the ground shake by jumping up and down as hard as you possibly can?
- ☐ Imagining what it would be like to ski down a gigantic sand dune?
- ☐ Playing with magnets and finding out what sticks and what doesn't?

then you might like to be a geophysical mathematician

DID YOU KNOW?

Geophysical mathematicians are a lot like geologists. Geologists try to understand how the Earth was made, what it is made out of, and how it has changed over time.

WHERE DO THEY WORK?

Geophysical mathematicians work in universities, research institutes, and laboratories. Some also work for the government.

OLIVIA the DATA ANALYST

The word data means a collection of facts. Data can be numbers of people, or cups of ice cream, or types of monkey: almost anything! Olivia is a data analyst, which means it is her job to make data easy to understand and work with.

For example, a company making chocolate bars might tell Olivia how many bars it sells each year, how much each bar costs to make, and how much they charge for each bar. Olivia then looks at this data and uses her maths skills to tell the company how they could make more money. Maybe the chocolate bars should cost more money. Or maybe there is a cheaper way to transport the bars so the company can sell them in more places.

Do you like...

☐ Typing the biggest number you can think of into a calculator and then seeing what happens when you multiply it by another number?
☐ Drawing a table with rows and columns and ticking off which members of your family like which types of food?
☐ Playing noughts and crosses?

then you might like to be a data analyst

DID YOU KNOW?

There are two main types of data. Qualitative data describes what things are like.
For example: "The house is big and beautiful."
Quantitative data describes how many things there are.
For example: "The house has ten windows."

WHERE DO THEY WORK?

There is a lot of data in the world. Data analysts work on computers in places where people need to understand their data. That could be in companies, libraries, airports, sports centres, hotels, schools, or shops.

ANANYA the ARTIFICIAL INTELLIGENCE SPECIALIST

Ananya tries to get computers to think like humans do. You know how you can look at your friends and tell them apart? Artifical intelligence specialists like Ananya design programmes so that computers can tell people apart, too. They can also make computers learn how to answer riddles and talk to people without a human helping them.

Ananya can program computers to respond to human voices, find underground water, oil, or gas, and even tell someone why they're sick.

Do you like...

- ☐ Imagining what it would be like if you could ask a computer to do all your homework for you?
- ☐ Dipping your fingers in ink and then making fingerprints all over a piece of paper?
- ☐ Asking questions to a phone and hearing it answer?

then you might like to be an artificial intelligence specialist

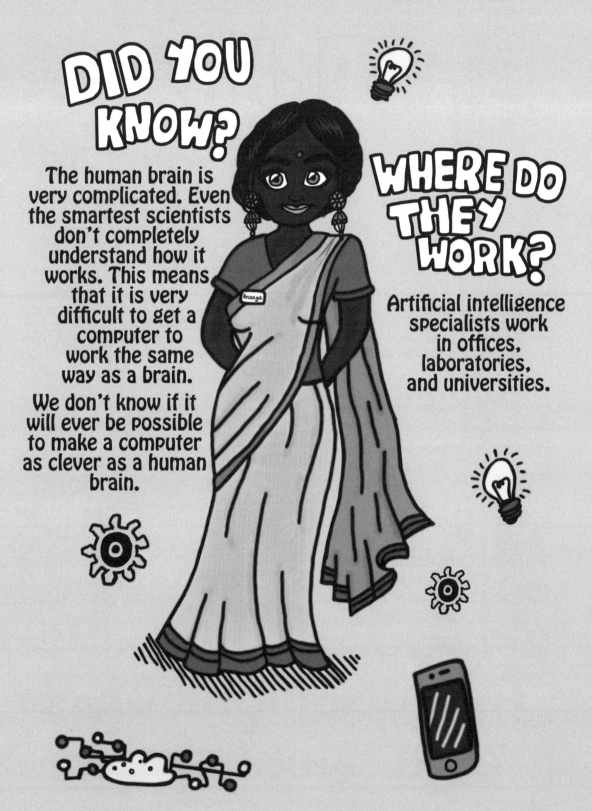

DID YOU KNOW?

The human brain is very complicated. Even the smartest scientists don't completely understand how it works. This means that it is very difficult to get a computer to work the same way as a brain.

We don't know if it will ever be possible to make a computer as clever as a human brain.

WHERE DO THEY WORK?

Artificial intelligence specialists work in offices, laboratories, and universities.

BOPHA the CRYPTOGRAPHER

Bopha uses maths to make secret codes called ciphers. Imagine that you want to send a secret message to your friend. If you write a letter, everyone will be able to read it. But if you come up with a secret code, only your friend will know what you are saying!

Bopha writes codes for messages sent over the internet. She takes normal messages and encrypts them, which means she uses maths to change them into code. Coded messages are called ciphertext.

Once a message has been delivered, it needs to be turned back into normal words. This is called decryption. Bopha is very good at both encryption and decryption. She helps make sure that important information stays safe on the internet.

Do you like...

☐ Making up passwords?
☐ Solving tricky maths problems?
☐ Coming up with secret words that only you and your friends know?

then you might like to be a cryptographer

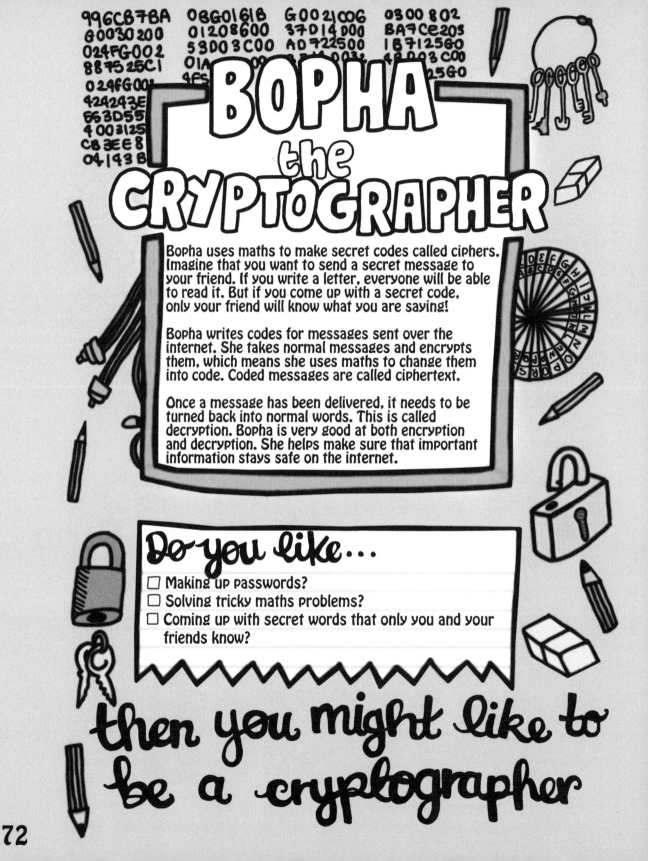

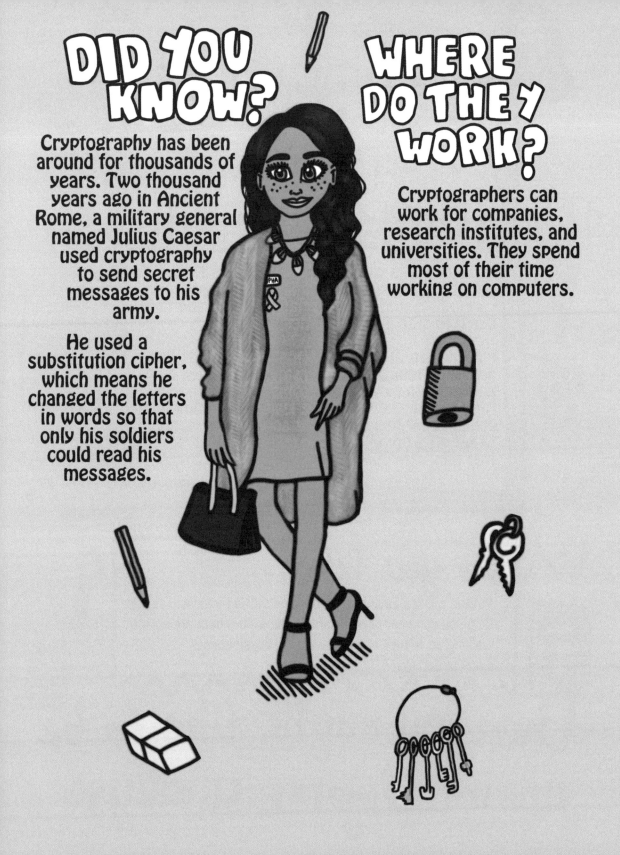

DID YOU KNOW?

Cryptography has been around for thousands of years. Two thousand years ago in Ancient Rome, a military general named Julius Caesar used cryptography to send secret messages to his army.

He used a substitution cipher, which means he changed the letters in words so that only his soldiers could read his messages.

WHERE DO THEY WORK?

Cryptographers can work for companies, research institutes, and universities. They spend most of their time working on computers.

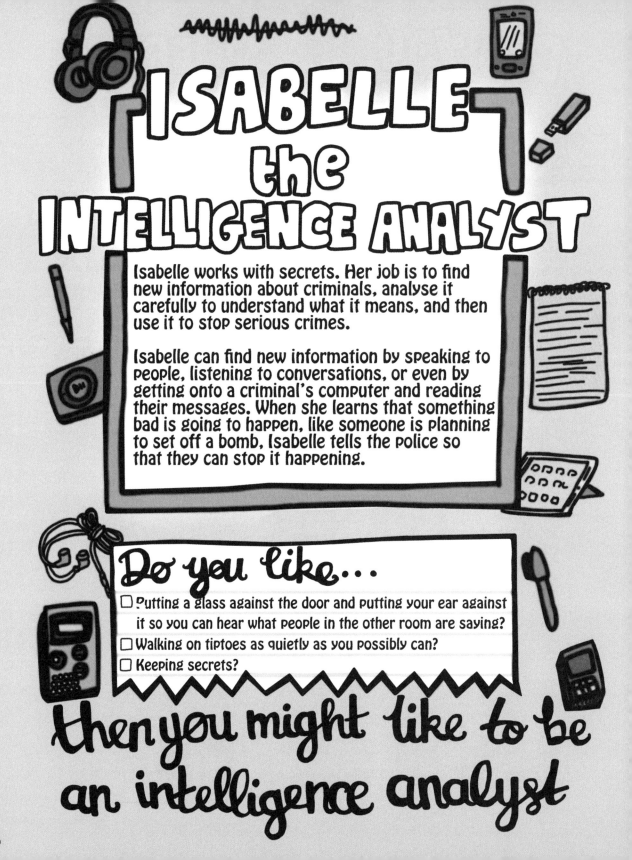

ISABELLE the INTELLIGENCE ANALYST

Isabelle works with secrets. Her job is to find new information about criminals, analyse it carefully to understand what it means, and then use it to stop serious crimes.

Isabelle can find new information by speaking to people, listening to conversations, or even by getting onto a criminal's computer and reading their messages. When she learns that something bad is going to happen, like someone is planning to set off a bomb, Isabelle tells the police so that they can stop it happening.

Do you like...

☐ Putting a glass against the door and putting your ear against it so you can hear what people in the other room are saying?

☐ Walking on tiptoes as quietly as you possibly can?

☐ Keeping secrets?

then you might like to be an intelligence analyst

DID YOU KNOW?

The word intelligence has two meanings. Sometimes, it means how clever somebody is.

For Isabelle's job, intelligence means a collection of information.

WHERE DO THEY WORK?

Intelligence analysts usually work for the government using special computers.

AVA the AIR TRAFFIC CONTROLLER

Ava works at the airport and helps planes take off and land safely. She uses special communication equipment to talk to pilots and give them advice.

Air traffic controllers like Ava also track the position of planes in the sky using radar. Radar stands for radio detection and ranging, and it uses radio waves to take pictures of the sky. Ava uses radar to help pilots to choose the best routes.

When planes are about to land at an airport, air traffic controllers like Ava organise the planes into a line and tell each pilot when it is safe to land. After a plane has landed, Ava also helps pilots park their planes.

Do you like....

☐ Getting your friend to shut their eyes and giving directions so they don't crash into furniture?

☐ Concentrating on something so hard that you completely forget where you are?

☐ Making paper aeroplanes and seeing how far you can get them to fly?

then you might like to be an air traffic controller

DID YOU KNOW?

There are three different types of air traffic controllers:

1. Area controllers track and guide planes while they are in the air.

2. Approach controllers manage planes as they get near to airports.

3. Aerodrome conrollers help pilots take off, land and park.

WHERE DO THEY WORK?

Air traffic controllers work in control towers at the airport. The control towers are very high up so the controllers can see all the runways. Area controllers and approach controllers also work at airports, usually in rooms called area control centres.

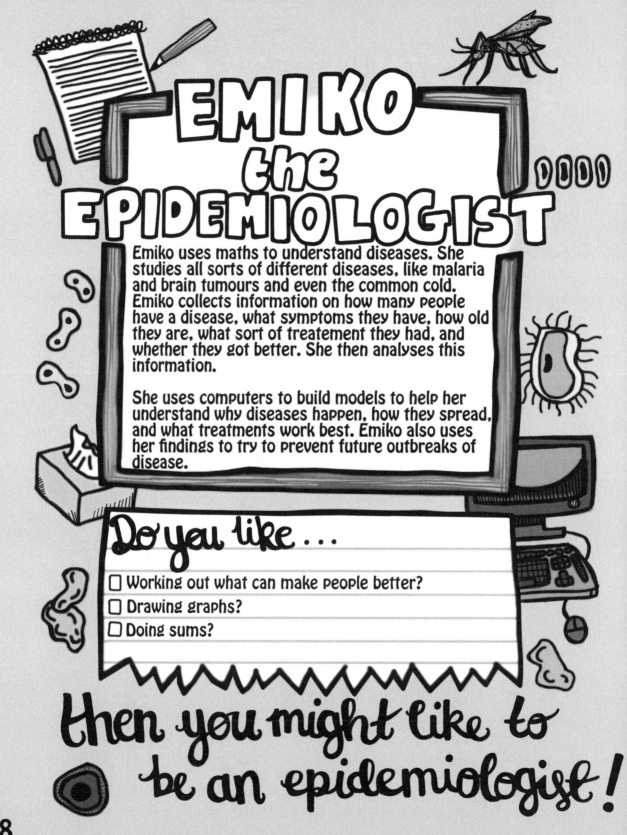

EMIKO the EPIDEMIOLOGIST

Emiko uses maths to understand diseases. She studies all sorts of different diseases, like malaria and brain tumours and even the common cold. Emiko collects information on how many people have a disease, what symptoms they have, how old they are, what sort of treatement they had, and whether they got better. She then analyses this information.

She uses computers to build models to help her understand why diseases happen, how they spread, and what treatments work best. Emiko also uses her findings to try to prevent future outbreaks of disease.

Do you like...

☐ Working out what can make people better?
☐ Drawing graphs?
☐ Doing sums?

then you might like to be an epidemiologist!

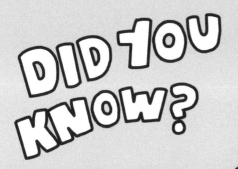

DID YOU KNOW?

Outbreaks of disease are called epidemics. This is where the name epidemiologist comes from.

WHERE DO THEY WORK?

Epidemiologists usually work in offices in universities and health centres. But sometimes they travel to different countries to collect new data.

Children who will CHANGE the world

Emily Anscombe
Jessica Anscombe
Olivia Armstrong
Edie Arthur
Francesca Arthur
Emina Aspbury
Sophie Bahl
Zanna Banks
Lily Barnes-Carson
Karli Basson
Joseph Bastian
Nadia Bates
Juliette Baudouin
Myrtille Baudouin
Jessica Cecily Jennet Bicknelle-Kendall
Oliver Stephen Peter Bicknelle-Kendall
Auden Billingsley
Anaïs Boettcher
Carmen Boettcher
Ava Boheim
Lara Boheim
Maya Boheim
George Boris
Adam Bridger

Thea Bridger
Georgia Blue Brown
Iris Byler
Liv Byrne
Isabella Coco Candy
Sophia Chloe Candy
Sadie Canty
Teddy Canty
Millie Cawkhill
Bella Charlier
Olivia Charlier
Amy Clarke
Oriana Coghill
Isabelle Cole
Rhiannon Cole
Isla Grace Connolly
Ella Cooke
Alice Cosserat
Isaac Cosserat
Eva Crewe
Beatrix Cross
Elektra Davenport
Kalypso Davenport
Millie Derow

Irene Donaghy
Gemma Donnellan
Eva Ella Beaux Dyer
Lily Florence Layla Dyer
Lucy Evans
Hanni Farley
Anna Fellows
Nina Fellows
Madeleine Finucane
Ceci Foan
Naomi Foan
Lucy Gallagher
Matilda George
Ned Gillard
Poppy Gillard
Iris Anne Ginns
Jessica Gould
Emilia Grantham
Katie Hackworth
Sophia Hackworth
Josephine Hall
Matilda Hall
Seungheon Han
Katia Walz Hardy
Rebecca Harvey
Amelia Hayes
Emma Helder
Bonnie Hewitt
Laura Hodds
Grace Holmes
Becky Hudson

Chloe Hughes
Isabelle Hughes
Leon Hughes
Polly Igoe
Clare Ilott
Eloise Ilott
Maya Khan
Freddie Kramer
Mathilda Kramer
Amelia Lam
Ariel Lam
Isadora Lands
Victoria Ludlow Lane
Kerri-Ann Larkin
Sehn Lathigra
Archie Lewis
Flora Lewis
Tilly Lewis
Juliette Li
Clement Longhurst
Rosie Longhurst
Dylan Louzado
Frankie Louzado
Georgie Louzado
Bram Mathew
Elva Mathew
Tom McCaig
Florence McCluskie
Oscar McCourt-Perfect
Lucy McGonigle
Louisa Molyneux

Anna Sequeira Morris
Caitlin Muir
Dillon Naik
Maya Naik
Natalie Newell
Saoirse Nic Niocaill
Isla Noonan
Elis Ooman
Lorcan Ooman
Harriet Orme
Elisabeth Orr
Beatrice Parmigiani-Donkin
Francesca Parmigiani-Donkin
George Parmigiani-Donkin
William Parmigiani-Donkin
Anna Nichols Popplewell
Theodore Poyet
Louis Poyet
Oscar Poyet
Isabel Price-Stephens
Joshua Price-Stephens
Phoebe Rankin
Poppy Rankin
Eleanor Jane Redfern
Chloe Repetto
Isla Ritchie
Olivia Rivera-Oughton
Lily Robinson
Max Schluechter
Mia Schluechter
Sydney Seeger

Arella Smith
Nina Starkey-Hughes
Ans Strobbe
Ward Strobbe
Thea Subritsky
Lorenzo Tonellotto
Emma Underhill
Henry Underhill
Madeleine Underhill
Lucy Veerhuis
Bethan Watson
Boris Watson-Hicks
Damon Watson-Hicks
Lois Weeks
Emily Jess Whiting
Max Whiting
Phoebe Whiting
Jack Wilkins
Cara Williams
Arianne Wilson
Gwen Wood
Clara Woodcraft
Hayley Yates
Annie Young
Emily Young

About the Author

Bryony Mathew is a British diplomat with a passion for inspiring children, especially girls, in the STEM fields (science, technology, engineering, and maths). She has travelled all over the world, from Zambia, Indonesia and the Democratic Republic of Congo to Greenland, Brazil and the Philippines. Bryony has held diplomatic positions in India and China; most recently, she was deputy ambassador to Cambodia. She has a PhD in neuroscience, an MSc in primate brain evolution, is a mum of two, and likes to run.

About the Illustrator

Millie Bicknelle is a Creative Writer and Illustrator currently based in London. Nothing gives her greater pleasure than bringing a writer's idea to life, giving the most imaginative, detailed and accurate representation of the characters they enjoyed inventing so much. She has travelled around the world, working with children in Spain, Greece, Canada, and even as an elf for Santa in Lapland. With her love for children and her love for stories, she decided to combine the two together and come back to London to work on Children's Books full time.

For Elva and Bram

A HUGE thank you to all the amazing Kickstarter backers who believed in this book and made it possible.

Copyright © Bryony Mathew, 2018

First edition

Published in the United Kingdom in 2018

No part of this publication may be reproduced, stored in a retrieval system, or transmitted, in any form, or by any means, electrical, mechanical, photocopying, recording or otherwise without the prior written permission of the author, Bryony Mathew.

Edited by Katherine Mechling

Printed in Italy by L.E.G.O. S.P.A.

A CIP catalogue record for this book is available from the British Library.

ISBN: 978-1-9164515-0-6

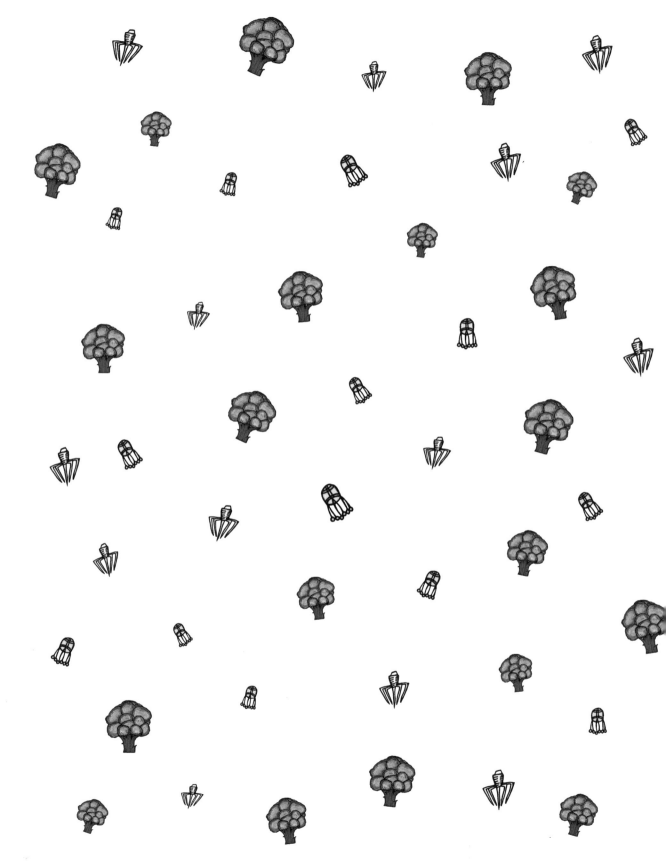